THE MAKING OF
TOM CAT

A FATHOM WIDE, TWO-PLUS LONG, AND HALF A FATHOM DEEP

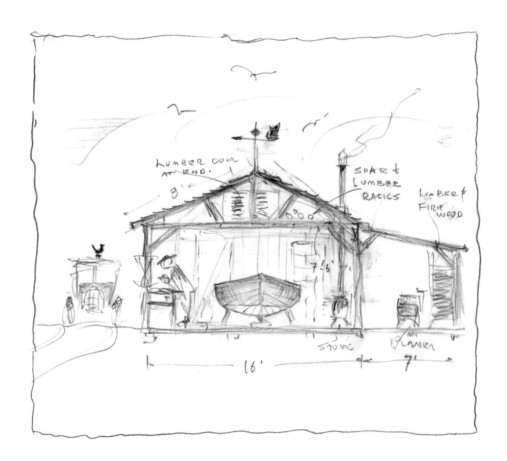

BY WILLIAM GARDEN

WoodenBoat Books

Published by WoodenBoat Publications, Inc.
Naskeag Road, PO Box 78
Brooklin, Maine 04616 USA
www.woodenboat.com

ISBN: 0-937822-78-7

First Printing 2004

Book design: Kat Stuart Design
Front cover and all drawings by William Garden
Photographs courtesy of William Garden

Printed in Canada by Friesens

Library of Congress Catalog-in-Publication Data on file

FOREWORD

"Our yachts are toy boats—the glint on a lovely brief bubble of time. A boat's importance as an escape from reality, as a change of pace, as a theme for reflection, and as an art form, gives it value."

—*From William Garden's book* Yacht Designs II

THERE'S NO ONE I know who likes to draw boats more than Bill Garden. A blank sheet of paper never fails to excite him for its creative possibilities. Over the course of his 86 years, Bill has filled thousands of blank sheets with every type and size of boat imaginable—from sailing canoes to ocean racers and from miniature tugboats to high-speed megayachts.

Most of my generation got to know the name William Garden through *The Rudder* or *Yachting* magazines where his designs of the 1940s and 1950s showed up in nearly every issue. Each boat was so handsome and depicted with such warmth and clarity that it would set you to dreaming. You could see yourself as the happy and contented pipe-smoking, sou'wester-clad skipper that Bill often showed at the helm. Or the guy who just finished painting the bottom of his grounded-out boat in one of Bill's perspective renderings. All this took place back when boats were simple and moderate-to-small in size, and the designs as Bill drew them made lots of sense. Seiners, tugboats, salmon trollers, and gillnetters as well as pleasure boats showed up on those pages, and I wasn't alone in seeking out each new issue as it arrived at the local library. Inspiration just leapt off those pages and into our memories!

More than that, those magazines played a major role helping that young and talented designer establish a reputation and attract a devoted following.

A Canadian by birth, Bill's family moved to Seattle via Portland, Oregon, in 1928 when Bill was 10 years old. In Seattle, he found himself surrounded by wooden boats of all kinds and sizes—and took full advantage of

...resourcefulness prevailed, and he and his chum John Adams found endless ways to mess around with small boats...

that wonderful environment. Money was scarce, but resourcefulness prevailed, and he and his chum John Adams found endless ways to mess around with small boats—converting whatever craft happened to be available so it would sail and they could go cruising. For them, life was nothing but swell in those early years, and full of adventure despite the Great Depression.

After graduation from high school in 1935 Bill signed on with the brand-new Edison Boatbuilding School, as enrollee number five, to study under respected Scottish boatbuilder J. B. Chambers. There he learned hands-on construction as well as theory. Following theory, he began designing boats professionally in 1938 at age 20, and a glance through his two books, *Yacht Design* and *Yacht Design II,* clearly shows Bill's amazing diversity. Throughout his career, Bill has built and owned boats—lots of them—but he still finds the small ones totally consuming.

Working professionally on occasion, but mostly filling his days now with pleasurable boat-related activity, Bill Garden lives on a fairytale island called Toad's Landing near Sidney, British Columbia, where his design

office has been located since he moved back to Canada 35 years ago. Among his recent activities, he designed, then built with his own hands, the first Tom Cat (named *Catspaw*) which he's tweaked to perfection. At 12'6", she's a dear little boat and one that we trust will provide the same level of joyous engagement for you as she has for Bill Garden.

Maynard Bray
Brooklin, Maine

HOW IT ALL BEGAN

SOME THREE OR FOUR years ago, our neighbor Dennis Kranz was having such good fun daysailing his jib-and-mainsail dinghy in the cove off our island that he inspired us to put our old sailing peapod back afloat to join in these short afternoon sails. Three minutes to get underway for a quick sail outmatches the 20 or 30 minutes it took to have our schooner off the dock to pick up what often proved to be a fickle breeze. So, after a bit, we also rigged up our 14' clinker-built skiff *Never-dun* with a daggerboard and a sprit-rigged mainsail and jib to add another member to the local daysailing fleet.

Three minutes to get underway for a quick sail outmatches the 20 or 30 minutes it took to have our schooner off the dock...

These small boats—about the minimum that one can climb aboard and sail off in—are bung-up with charm. They're the next size up from sailing pond models, but here, aside from standing on deck and gripping a shroud for a sweep of the horizon, we can emulate Stuart Little in a small boat that one can actually hop into, donning a ribboned sailor hat, set up the sprit or hoist away on the halyard, and then, with the mainsheet trimmed, bear off for that wonderful feeling as the sail fills, and the bow wave starts its chuckle, and the wee boat comes to life.

Certainly, tacking up a wooded shoreline on a fresh morning breeze in an open sailboat must be one of the all-time highs for the dedicated waterman. First we head off with an inshore tack with a lovely shoreline to contemplate as we work up along the beach, then over to the offshore tack with its great sweep of horizon ahead. Maybe starboard-tack a duck or accomplish some other brave deed; then, with the peak *just right* for a perfect set of the sail, off it is around the headland on a great close reach as she slides along at the three knots that feels like eight.

During a couple of summers of sailing these dinghies, our thoughts turned toward what might be an ideal small sailing boat for our summer's light-weather area here in the Gulf Islands off Canoe Cove, British Columbia. Some sort of boat with elbow room for two, and light to handle. She'd be an unballasted centerboarder with a non-fouling rudder for

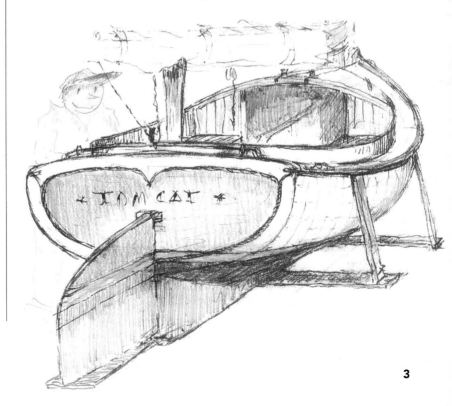

sliding through the prevalent kelp patches off our island, which we call Toad's Landing (see WoodenBoat magazine Nos. 60 and 166); all this plus a high ratio of sail area to wetted surface to ensure a good drifter. A little catboat seemed to suit these particulars and brought to mind the 12' Beetle Cat (see WB Nos. 51–53), which looked to be ideal for the young and limber.

So it came to pass that all sorts of Beetle data was exhumed, and Dennis was off on a Beetle hunt to replace his jib-and-mainsail boat. But we seemed to be a Beetle-free coast. Lots of dead-end leads were chased down, and then other island neighbors also got steamed up Beetle-wise. So the search turned eastward to the thick of catboat country, New England, where Maynard Bray helped Dennis find two Beetle Cats to ship west. Beetle #1812, named *Overture*, was one. The other, in better shape and needing only a normal cosmetic cleanup, was renamed *Top Cat*— although *Overture* thought this a bit much. With a couple of little orphan Beetles scheduled to come west the following spring, we decided to work up plans for a Beetle-sized catboat of our own to build here at Toad's Landing over the winter—a boat with raised seating, for more comfort. (The leg cramps generated from sitting on the floorboards can

take the sparkle out of a good sail.) Although this was the number one requirement, the following considerations also came to mind for the design of Tom Cat:

- A high sail area–to–wetted surface ratio, at least matching that of a Beetle.
- A tumblehome stem with a slightly hollow waterline to best work through our short chop or summertime powerboat wake.
- Some exposed keel for beaching and directional stability with the centerboard raised.
- A non–fouling barn–door rudder with end plates for a real bite when broad-reaching in a breeze.
- A hole through the stem at waterline height for towing without broaching and overturning.
- Freeboard enough for a dry boat and to allow for the cockpit seats.
- An under–deck stowage area for life jackets, picnic basket, and miscellaneous gear.

So the design was worked up and construction went on as time allowed and winter turned to spring. But still no sign of *Top Cat* and *Overture*. At last the long wait ended. The month of June saw an 18–wheeler come rolling down the road to Canoe Cove after a hard voyage westbound across Canada with a big

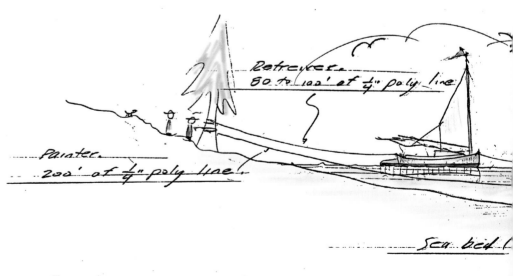

Sketch plan of Beaching Gear.

sailboat onboard and two small Beetles poked under its bilge—an indignity furthered by the Beetles having ridden the whole weary distance stern-first. There was much to do in putting things shipshape, and then a get-together on shore at Toad's Landing to welcome the immigrant Beetles to our waters, complete with a barbecue and speeches to put them at ease. Here's the welcoming speech:

"Beetle lore tells us that some four score years ago there was born on the far-off New England shore a small catboat, conceived by Elder Beetle and dedicated to the proposition that the time had come to create from a small pile of lumber and canvas the most possible fun to be had for boys and girls of all ages, a boat within the least practical dimensions that would furnish accommodations for a crew of four, or for singlehanding, while giving pleasure and a chuckle to all who beheld her small, rotund, pancake-like form.

"We are come on this auspicious occasion to welcome to Western waters two small immigrant Beetles. Wee cats with the courage and audacity to make the long, arduous passage over what must have been a seemingly endless portage, buoyed up by the hope of a friendly welcome from their airman mariner sponsor, who we must now applaud…[pause for heavy applause]… who also through the kindness of his heart and deep pockets…[more applause, whistles, and foot stamping]… caused to have his own Beetle accompanied by a small older sister, who, despite being in need of boatyard attention, had bravely faced the awesome westbound transit. [Pause for crowd and applause to settle down.]

"We are fortunate to have these newcomers sailing in our Western waters, bleak I'm sure, and strange without a fleet of fellow Beetles bobbing happily nearby. But I trust that the new young gaffer soon to be laancht… [Downeast pronunciation here to give the Beetles a feeling of security]… will help ease homesickness. Soon the little cats will go scunning along our island shores in a nice flag-snappin' breeze, with the travails of the past long forgotten. [Cheers, some claps and sobs.]

"Three cheers and hats in air." [Heavy cheering while we do the crowd for handclasps and back-slaps. One chap of literary bent remarked, "You girls done good on that awesome transit bit."]

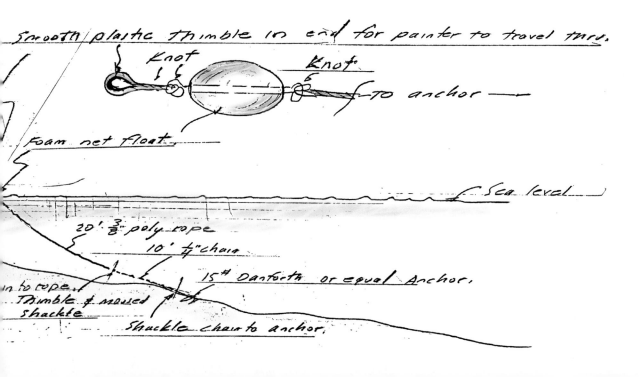

LETTERS HOME

AN EXPLANATION

WE'LL GO OFF now to some of the further adventures of the small immigrant Beetle girls *Top Cat* and *Overture* (*Ovie* for short) as outlined in the following two letters written by the now-Western Beetles' spokesgirl, *Top Cat*, to their faraway Downeast sisters.

Top Cat, the younger Beetle sister who traveled west with *Ovie*, as you will note from the occasional lapse in grammar, has a rather common way of expressing herself. *Overture*, Hull #1812, her older sister, I find is somewhat snooty, more assured of her position, and apparently not as interested in the general run of younger Beetles—hence, the delegation of correspondence. *Ovie*, I'm told, was often dismayed by the rowdy, around-the-buoys razzle-dazzle of racing. Although a fleet champion

one year, she intimated that she mainly sailed ahead to avoid the crowd and members of a fleet that she didn't wish to know.

For those who question the interpretation of these letters home, it seems that boats built of wood maintain a communication beyond most folks' hearing or understanding, and, as in our own language, they have a somewhat diverse way of expressing themselves depending upon their type and background. But they have equally bigoted outlooks, just as we do, on many things. For instance, on boats of a petroleum derivative, the wooden ones, proud of their forest background, often refer to the fiberglass ones generically as having come out of an oil can or glue pot. The interpretation of their letters, although I'm sure with some errors on my part, often has had to be toned down or have an occasional

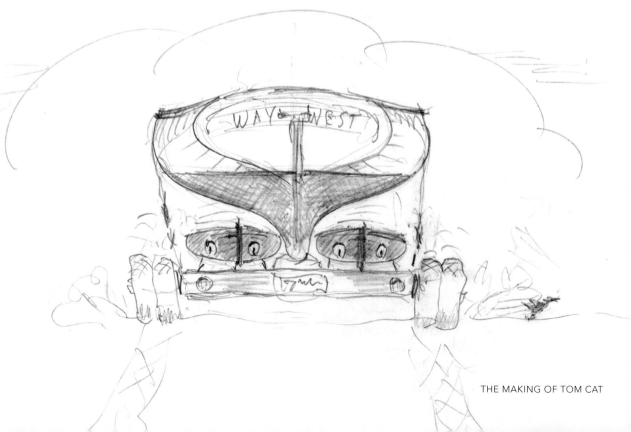

paragraph deleted when, as in *Top Cat*'s case, she goes more or less bigotty overboard, complaining that the plastic boats are forever mentioning that they don't leak, which usually stirs up her rebuttal about cookie-cutter clones conceived on a keyboard. As she says, "Any one of us Beetles, although of an admittedly patrician model" (I liked that), "at least show dissimilar tool marks." I must say, though, that our own *Catspaw* seems to maintain her dignity even when some grossly misshapen three-story motorboat snowplows by. This is probably due to her good genes— and being reinforced with biaxial roving.

I suppose if one doesn't hear the boats talk, one either hasn't listened long enough or hasn't paid proper attention. I've been somewhat upset about being questioned as to the accuracy of my interpretation of the Beetle letters. As the Beetles will certainly confirm,

any misinterpretation has at all times been scrupulously adhered to. Originally I thought it would be a breach of privacy to publish their letters. However, after much soul searching (about a half minute), it seemed my duty to pass them along for the edification of those folks who, I'm told, are completely unaware of the vast catboat culture. The Beetles have even mentioned that in their territory back East, when making an introduction, one often hears "Hello, I'm so-and-so, Beetle number 1620 (or whatever), Haaaaarvard '82." So we have the greeting, the name, and an indication of good judgment, followed by scholastic background. Anyway, at least, that's what I was told.

So on to the first letter home to Eastern Beetles, which *Top Cat* started to edit and then got grumpy. [The occasional lapses in spelling and proper grammar are certainly not *Ovie's*.]

Dear Beetles,

   Me and 'Overture' have been real busy since being sold, as it were, out west. Much has happened since we were tied down on that truck and brought out here backwards after a last look back at the dear old Atlantic. Do you know we haven't seen a lobster since Blue Hill, but lots of crabs out here, big Dungeness honkers and neat little spider crabs that hang on to kelp fronds as we go slippin' by overhead. You must have thought that we had ended up as flower boxes full of dirt by now, but the trip West was admittedly some spooky. Huckledy-buck out of Brooklin backwards on a big truck with more tires than plenty, and ended up stuffed port and starboard under the bilges of a plastic sloop. All the way out here looking at where we came from. Canada is some wide place, and it would probably half fill the Atlantic if it was blowed east in a good smart breeze. Poor Ovie, scared stiff at sum of our fast clips crossing the prairies when the steerer man shook out a reef and really gave the truck a rap full.

   Nice folks out here though, but kind of weird. They met us at this place called Canoe Cove. Folks have funny accents but mostly well meaning and we gathered a good crowd of admirers, but not a mention by anyone of having gone to Harvard. Some comments didn't go over too well with Ovie. Buxom was somewhat overdone but also good comments on our wetted surface and sail area ratios, so me and Ovie really clammed up. But Ovie's seams were dried out and she swamped when put overboard. So embarrassed in front of all those people that when she was towed out to Toad's Landing for a fix-up, she just filled up and rolled over. Poor thing, but old Bill rolled her back and triced her up close to his launch Merlin who is an elegant old hard worker with a handsome canoe stern. Really quite Edwardian handsome with a nice sheer. Imagine, still hustling around at age 99, sort of like Olin. But old Bill was cussing the lack of a down-low towing ring on Ovie, so we didn't have time to chat. Ovie got hauled up right off in the Toad's Landing shop where a nice couple, Grant and Heather are their names, pitched right in and tidied things up with all new paint and stuff.

Me and Ovie are hauled out for the off-season now cause God-parents Dennis and Teri go off to crocodile country in the S'east where they spend winters with a bunch of airplanes. Dennis started out in sailplanes and then on to ones with lots of motors. He is always squinting at our sails. Little halyard winches have been fitted on our foredecks for peak tweaking and throat adjustment. These guys out here are sure quick off the line in buying us nice stuff. I got rechristened "Top Cat" which Ovie thinks is a little much, but fits Capt. Dennis who is a goer & speed nut. Once old Bill took us to weather in his cat while chewing on a chicken leg, next thing I knew Dennis had ordered me a dandy new Doyle sail. Just heard that Ovie is having new deck canvas and coamings this winter. Pete, our paid hand and friend, will put it on over a thin glued-down plywood overlay. Some good job!

Lots of good sailing days here in winter but good to be up on our trolley under a tarp or up in our boat shed, where Ovie is getting fixed. Our boss built us a neat boat hoist on rails. Flat deck and a slick way to come up for a scrub or winter rest. Hoist is on the west side of our island with a view looking north 30 miles or so to a mountain range. Big honkers, not the humps we had Downeast. Another major range is across the straits that we see when sailing to the southard, and fresh air although this is a light-air area. Fresh air, not the reused New York City stuff we often get blowing Downeast. Fresh enough to chew, Ovie says, as fresh air from all the way across the Pacific Ocean comes tickling along our reef-points.

Ovie says to tell you that the kelp here starts down 30 feet, big suckers like we've never seen with long leaves off the kelp heads. With the board up we can skin right over them. Must make the codfish blink to see us squirt on by.

Leaving home from dear old Maine waters backwards on a truck was as hard on us as broaching, losing a mast, or ending up swamped with our loose gear blowing off seaward to England. But we like it here. Ovie keeps me company, and old Bill on the next island (Toad's Landing, he calls it) out the Bay from us has a nice cat, called Catspaw, for us to sail with. A little plush for my liking with go-fast doodads and lots of brightwork, but a nice enough boat that keeps us on our toes when sailing together.

Catspaw gets hoisted out and launched on a bridle that dangles from a nice boom on Toad's dock. Has a nice little electric winch with remote control so we all sail with clean scrubbed bottoms. Some folks from Maine were here last summer and one old geezer was sailing Ovie. Capt. Page I think was his name, a neat guy. Diaphone larynx he had, and it looked like little Ovie was sliding along with a big old lobster at the helm. But what a treat to hear a proper accent! Ovie felt right at home. These guys out here have us all in good trim, and do a lot of experimenting with sail draft and stuff so our sailing is always interesting. Last winter Ovie was hauled out in Bill's shop, some good place, for new guards and more painting work by Grant and Heather, so with this winter's work she'll look some wicked good when Peter has her new decks and coamings done. Capt. Dennis Kranz likes things in top shape. With that new sail for me, my old good sail was passed on to Ovie. Nice full easy draft for the light-air summers out here. We got rid of our mast hoops; old what's-his-name Bill over at Toad's Landing rigged us up with lacing so the hoist goes up and down like a 5 pound lead. Our sails stay bent on all the time out here, so we have cod line lacing on boom and gaff for quick and easy head and foot adjustment. A nice little thumb cleat to gather the luff lacing when the sail is lowered, so no hang-ups. Little snubbing winches handle the halyards so once they are around the windward mark, they are quick to ease off the peak to get rid of the off-the-wind wrinkle. Then it's up with the board, and away we go, smart as paint.

We've made a good friend in Bill's little Catspaw (she's his Tom Cat design, so we've heard). Nice to sail with, and we've heard that a story about her building was in the WoodenBoat magazine. Quite a handsome cat, with a very refined manner and pure luxury to sail, with regular stern sheets and seats, all with cushions plus cushioned coamings for backrests. Old Bill denies himself absolutely nothing onboard Catspaw. He has go-ashore knee boots chocked off on brass hooks in the neat little cuddy, with a railway net for stowage of oilskins and all sorts of bottles and secret stuff.

That's all for now.
Love, Top Cat

Dear Atlanticers,

No word back yet from my letter to you eastern Beetles, but anyway… Ovie is out of her repairwork and sort of lording it over me with her new deck & coamings. Capt. Kranz had the coamings shipped out from the Beetle shop, pre-bent, and they fit some good. Pete even ran all of her bronze fittings and her name letters over the buffer at Toad's Landing. My hardware all slated for the same polishing soon.

Poor little Ovie says she took a fair amount of thumping during her operation. Her patchwork cedar deck was all faired off nice and smooth, then an 1/8" plywood deck was glued down over it prior to laying new deck canvas. To take the coamings, the inboard face of the cockpit had some unfairness dressed off to a nice, fair line so the coamings went on without the sort of farm-style quarter-round gap-hiding moldings. She looks some nice. Just a neat bead of Sikaflex, they called the stuff, was run in to form a little fillet where the deck meets the coaming. Ovie says they ran the bead with a scary-looking sort of a bug killer gun and smoothed it out with a wet finger. Ovie also got a neat wooden mast collar ring. They made one for me too, so when my boss gets back north again we'll both look nice painted now with the same colors. Ovie's transom is white again, bottom green, white topsides, varnished oak trim and Beetle orange buff decks. We both got new sheets and halyards from Charlie York at Beetle Inc. Came from England, I'm told. Feels nice on my sheaves and looks proper. Same stuff on Bill's Catspaw. He says it's swell. So we're all ready for the boss when he gets home. Both he and Teri, his crew and tactician, will be very pleased with us as top-of-the-line cats.

Later on I'll get to chat with the nice local boats that I hear have had some interesting experiences, but first a snort of creosote oil, then a few weeks of hibernation on my chocks—padded, mind you, no more being stacked up on our transoms out here!

Your friend,
Top Cat

EDITORIAL NOTE: It seems that *Top Cat* knocked out the above letter, in a hurry, late last winter in order to get it off before the U.S. postage rate increase from 69 to 80 cents went into effect. She grumbled something about the government needing money to pay for the oil war. *Top Cat* was a Democrat prior to her forced Canadian allegiance. *Overture*, I assume is a Republican. Both aver to having been scared into rescinding their U.S. citizenship during a truck stop en route west when some hunters tried to pull them off the truck and stuff them with straw to use as duck blinds. I understand that the matter has been turned over to the State Department to sort out.

With the Beetles here and ceremoniously settled in at Canoe Cove and with about a month to go to the first Tom Cat's launching, we'll back up to the preceding winter to tell the story of Tom's design and construction.

TOM CAT

DESIGNING AND BUILDING TOM CAT

WITH TOM'S REQUIREMENTS in mind, some sketches were roughed out to put form to the small cat, then on with the engrossing steps of developing some numbers to guide the design concept to reality.

Tom's need for raised seating required a greater depth of hull and more freeboard than that of a Beetle, resulting in Tom being more of a small ship. Tom's displacement and interior volume are about one-and-a-half times that of a Beetle, with the ratio of sail area to wetted surface being a close match. Tom's 120 sq. ft.

"Tom's displacement and interior volume are about one-and-a-half times that of a Beetle."

of sail area relative to its heavier displacement seems to be about right, although the calculations suggested the heavier-displacement hull could take 130 sq. ft. of sail area to the Beetle's 112 (see Performance, page 36). Anyway, as things turned out, the boats seem well matched in our non-bloodthirsty local sailing. (Since adding a cuddy cabin last winter, I'm now going to demand a *cruising* cat's time allowance. However, being a thoroughly sportsmanlike chap, I'll only call for this when *Catspaw*—the name we chose for our own Tom Cat—is trailing.)

From the above requirements, drawings were developed for the construction of a traditional, carvel-planked boat over either steam-bent or laminated frames. Meanwhile, lots of bits and

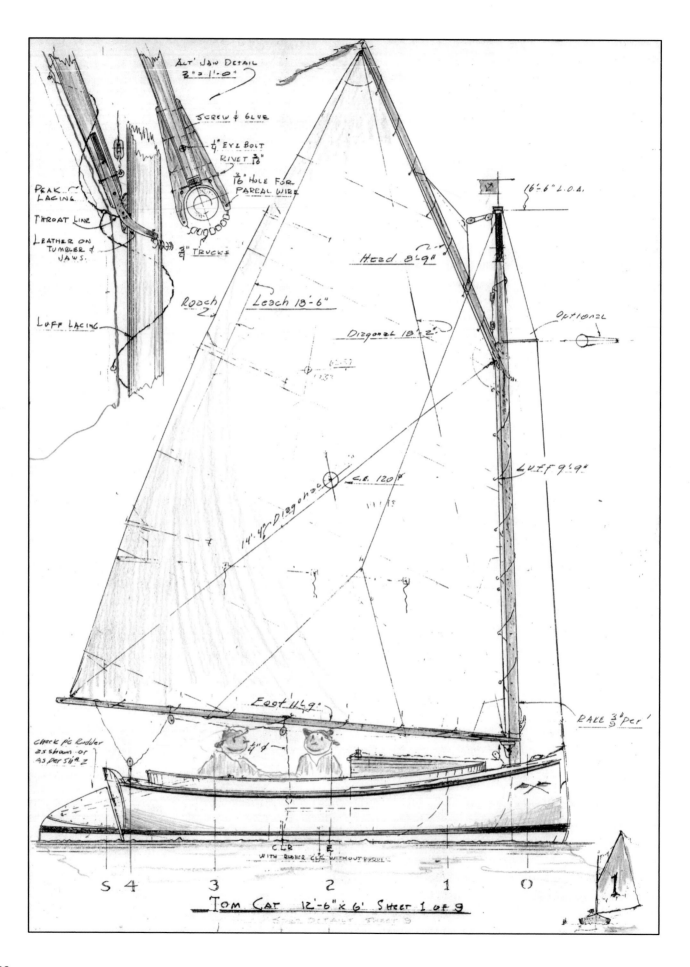

ALT' JAW DETAIL
3" = 1'-0"

SCREW & GLUE

1/4" EYE BOLT

RIVET 3/16"

3/16" HOLE FOR
PARREL WIRE

PEAK
LACING

THROAT LINE

LEATHER ON
TUMBLER &
JAWS.

3/4" TRUCKS

LUFF LACING

Roach
2"

Leach 18'-6"

Head 8'-9"

Diagonal 18'-2"

16'-6" L.O.A.

Optional

LUFF 9'-9"

14'-4" Diagonal

C.E. 120 □'

RAKE 3/8" PER 1'

Foot 11'-9"

Check for Rudder
as shown or
as per sheet

4"d

CLR   E
WITH RUDDER C.L.R. WITHOUT RUDDER

S 4   3   2   1   O

TOM CAT 12'-6" x 6' SHEET 1 of 9

1

pieces were collected. Friends, in a burst of enthusiasm for duplicate Tom Cats, laminated a half dozen oak stems before to deciding to build larger catboats, hence one of these stems plus a pile of beautiful Western red cedar from Octopus Point showed up at Toad's Loading. Tom was about to take form. So, now off to the shop.

BUILDING CATSPAW

First, the lines plan was drawn out full-size on the shop floor. Then the station molds were cut out from 3/4" pine shelving stock—the plank, frame, and ribband thickness having first been deducted from the body plan stations (which are drawn to the *outside* of planking). The molds were then set up on the building jig, along with the transom (which has only the plank thickness deducted) and the stem (which secures to its own vertical strongback).

The ribbands (see photo gallery, page 46) were next to go on, and were made from flat-grained, clear, full-length stock to ensure fair bending. Then the frame positions were marked on the ribbands and the steamed frames bent into place over them.

STRIP-PLANKING OPTION

The boat can also be strip-planked as an alternative to traditional carvel construction. In this case, the mold deduction would be made only for the plank thickness—the planks themselves being equivalent to ribbands and serving to guide the laminated bent frames, which go in after the boat is all planked and turned upright. There are many ways to build a boat, but in any case, if you take all possible care in initially lining things up, you'll avoid eyeballing and building-in eventual problems. *continued on page 15* ➤

PLANK WIDTHS USING THE BOSTON SCALE

To find the widths of hull planks at various bow-to-stern locations, a "Boston Scale" batten about 1/8" x 1" x 40" is made and calibrated to form a full-scale guide when bent along the frames over the curve of the hull. For an example, after the garboard and sheerstrakes have been spiled and fitted, there remains a maximum half-hull girth of 36" when measured around the curve of the bilge. Divided by eight planks per side, this results in 4½" maximum width. The hull girths will taper significantly toward the ends of this rotund shape, so a planking width scale to match the taper is marked as follows, based, in this case, on eight planks and a maximum girth of 36":

36" girth ÷ 8 planks = 4½" width
32" girth ÷ 8 planks = 4" width
28" girth ÷ 8 planks = 3½" width
24" girth ÷ 8 planks = 3" width
20" girth ÷ 8 planks = 2½" width
16" girth ÷ 8 planks = 2" width

Now, from the end of the batten, measure along 16" and mark and label a 2" crossing, at 20" a 2 ½" crossing, etc., all along the batten up to 36" and 4½". Then divide the distances between into

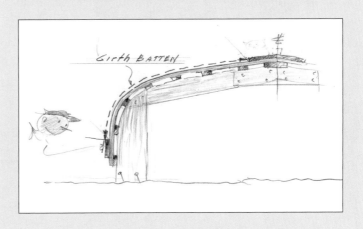

BOSTON SCALE continued...

fractions as noted on the sketch (below) to complete the batten scale. To use the Boston Scale batten, butt the zero end of the batten against the edge of the sheerstrake, bend it around the turn of the bilge, and at any point read off the plank width where the batten scale crosses the garboard. For a small boat, to best utilize the widths thus found, a plank pattern equal to the length of the boat as measured around a bilge diagonal is made from 1/4" plywood, one edge of which is straight and the other edge curved per the widths found by means of the planking scale. (Note that this pattern is only for plank widths; the edge curve or shape of each plank must be spiled from

the adjacent plank to get its shape. Past issues of *WoodenBoat* have much on spiling technique.) With the curve of a spiled plank's edge established from the spiling board, the other edge of the plank can be marked by tracing the plank pattern's width's so they follow the curve of the spiled line. Edge-setting, although tempting, must be minimized with light planking like Tom Cat's. Here, the ratio of thickness to width is 11%. On heavier work with a ratio of perhaps 40%, a long run of steamed planking can be advantageously wedged into a strong edge-set without problems.

Back for a moment to the Boston Scale: On a

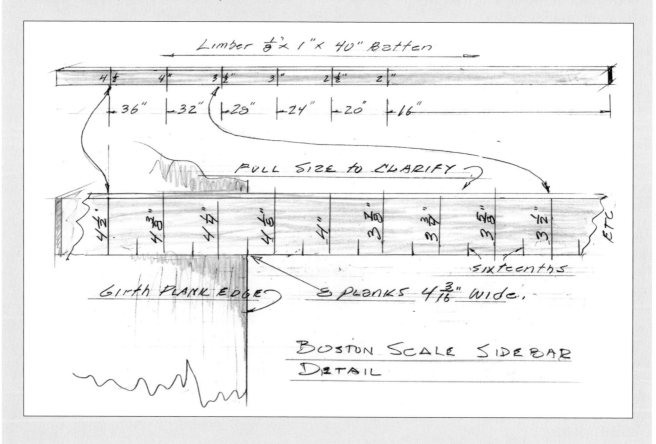

large boat the plank widths can be marked out on the back of a cloth measuring tape, then, with the eye hooked over a nail at the plank above, the tape stretched down around the bilge and the plank widths at this and other locations noted. In this case, the line of the garboards, broad-strakes, and walestrakes would have been established, along with a rough shell expansion to locate butts to yield a reasonably accurate lumber order.

The name "Boston Scale" was what Jim Chambers called this planking scale when I was shown it 70 years ago, and I've never thought much as to its origin. Probably it was known as the Cairo Scale two or three thousand years ago.

WoodenBoat has published articles on strip-planked construction (see WB Nos. 57 and 124), so there's no need to go into detail here. One important point is to cover the mold edges with narrow strips of plastic sheeting to avoid accidentally gluing the planking to the molds. Once the planking is in place, the hull is dressed off and faired up, then given an outer skin of biaxial fiberglass cloth set in epoxy resin. Thickened epoxy fills the weave, after which it is faired again and given another sanding. Then the boat is rolled over, with the molds still in place, onto a cradle. The molds are next removed, the interior dressed off, and the laminated frames sprung into place and epoxied together—again, over a plastic sheet—then later removed so that they can be smoothed up before being permanently epoxied into place. The strip-planked, edge-glued hull needs only about a half dozen more-or-less evenly spaced frames between the stem and the transom.

CARVEL PLANKING OPTION

For our own little carvel-planked *Catspaw*, we installed longitudinal ribbands (see pages 46 and 47) over the molds, followed by transverse steamed frames bent around the ribbands. Then she was planked up conventionally. The planks were fitted wood-to-wood inboard with a normal caulking seam outboard. But in lieu of wedging or the normal cotton caulking, the faired-off planking was given a coat of epoxy, after which all the seams and screw holes were filled with a mix of epoxy and microballoons before sheathing the hull with epoxy and biaxial cloth.

The plank seams could be traditionally caulked with cotton and puttied with seam compound, but the soft Western red cedar or Eastern white cedar planking is a worry when pulling up on a rough beach. The

BUILDING FORM SETUP

The mold detail drawing (sheet 8) shows the backbone assembled over the previously erected molds. First the stem is placed and braced 'thwartship as shown. Then the station molds are set up and the centerline apron is sprung over them from the stem to the forward face of the transom, and we're ready for the ribbands as shown at the upper right of the drawing. Note that the ribband below the sheer will help retain the topside shape. In bending the frames, having two people will work best, one each side, the frame positions having been previously marked on the ribbands. A frame, hot from the steambox, is pushed through between the apron and the ribbands, then bent down over the molds and secured in position. Prior to steaming, each frame should be marked so its flat grain goes against the ribbands. About 45 minutes of hot, wet steam will be needed, with the oak fresh from an overnight soaking. The corners of each frame should have a light sanding beforehand to minimize slivers, which can form a stress point leading to a break.

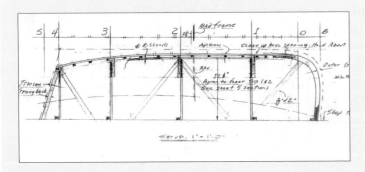

epoxy skin forms a tough membrane to help with chafe, plus it provides a leak-proof hull. Also, thickened epoxy pressed and knifed into the seams, in lieu of cotton and seam compound, is an excellent shell stiffener that resists the torsional load of the mast's heeling moment working against the righting moment of the crew's weight to windward. For a boat that lands on a beach, an even heavier fiberglass skin, plus fixed bilge keels, could be fitted—or, best of all, string her out on an outhaul that's rigged to an anchor as shown on the sketch on pages 4 and 5.

Each of the 1/2" cedar planks was steamed and cupped at each frame using cupping blocks as shown on sheet 3, which cause a steamed plank to follow the curve of the frames. This avoids the "backing-out," or hollowing, that is otherwise necessary on the inboard face of heavier planking to make it conform to the curvature of the frames. Each of the cupping blocks has holes bored through it to allow the fastenings to be driven without removing the blocks or clamps. Prior to steaming, each plank was sanded on its inboard face and given a coat of flat paint. The steam-bent frames were also painted, so that the inside of the hull is completely primed under the frames.

CENTERBOARD TRUNK

The inside of the centerboard trunk is usually neglected, so Tom's trunk sides are set back to widen the slot. For painting, the cover can be unscrewed to allow easy access. While the hull is still upside down but not yet fiberglassed, the centerboard slot should be cut through the keel, the planking, the apron, and the frames. This will allow the hull sheathing to carry down into the slot and seal the exposed edges of the planking and apron.

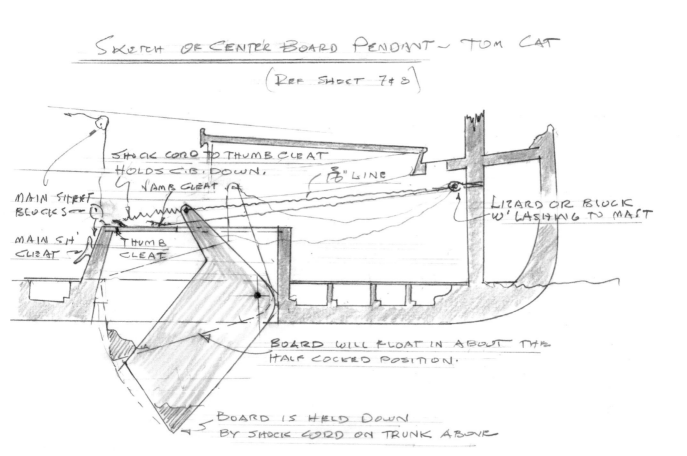

SKETCH OF CENTER BOARD PENDANT ~ TOM CAT

(REF SHEET 7 & 8)

SHOCK CORD TO THUMB CLEAT
HOLDS C.B. DOWN.

1½" LINE

JAMB CLEAT

LIZARD OR BLOCK
W' LASHING TO MAST

MAIN SHEET
BLOCKS

MAIN SH'T
CLEAT

THUMB
CLEAT

BOARD WILL FLOAT IN ABOUT THE
HALF COCKED POSITION.

BOARD IS HELD DOWN
BY SHOCK CORD ON TRUNK ABOVE

After the hull has been turned upright and set on a cradle, the frames are cut back for the centerboard trunk bedlogs and the fiberglass is trimmed flush with the top of the apron. The bedlogs are laid in bedding compound and screwed up from the bottom through the keel, planking, and apron. Gum or a worm-resistant hardwood is specified for the bedlogs and is a good choice for the internal cheek pieces as well. Next come the floor timbers, the cabin bulkhead, the sheer clamps, etc. As soon as they are fitted, she's ready for the deck work as noted on the drawings.

THE RIG

Those who complete the work this far will find the outboard joinery to be all downwind work, so let's go over the rig, which consists of a single mast, a boom and a gaff, one sail, two halyards, a headstay, mainsheet, and lazy-jacks—plus the all-important masthead wind fly. Short of a jibheaded main, this rig is about as simple as we can get. The mast is of spruce or Douglas-fir and can be either solid, in which case the diameter will be 3¼", or hollow with a diameter of 3½" and a wall thickness of 5/8". These options are shown on the plans and described in the mast sidebar beginning on page 27. The boom and gaff are solid. The boom has simple jaws that land on a half-circle bolster epoxied to the

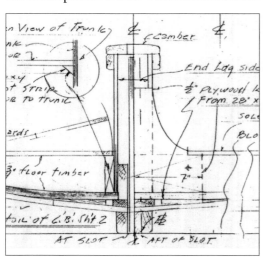

continued on page 19 ➤

WOODEN CLEATS

The general lead of sheets and halyards can be found on the drawings. For those who prefer the feel and look of wooden cleats, the sketches herewith will provide an interesting project in the outfitting of Tom.

The mainsail can be trimmed with a simple wooden cleat or one of the excellent but costly, sheave-and-cam-cleat combinations that are on the market. Should a wooden mainsheet cleat be preferred, the sketch outlines an interesting one made of hardwood or, better yet, from a natural crook of yew or juniper. Work it up, smooth the corners to minimize chafe, and the result will be a tough, handsome, easy-on-the-eyes cleat. I almost added "and a joy forever"—well, perhaps some rapture might be involved after the first few coats of varnish. In any case, this will be a far better product than some of the ridiculous radiator-ornament, decorator-inspired, rope-destroying cleats on the market today.

Back to the mainsheet: On any small boat, it's a line that seldom should be belayed and is best nipped under the thumb of a cleat, then to your hand, pending the need to ease her through a puff. For Tom Cat, the hauling part of the mainsheet will lead

from the block on the centerboard trunk, down under the cleat, then to your hand as described above or simply passed under, led upwards and into the jamb slot of the cleat as shown on the sketch—where a quick jerk will release it. This forked jamb cleat works so well on our *Catspaw* that my chums Loop and Ross used it for a simple sand-casting pattern by plugging up the slot to draw and poured some in bronze. For these metal jamb cleats, a 1/8" hole drilled at the base of where you want the slot to be serves as a target for hacksawing, after which the slot is filed smooth for

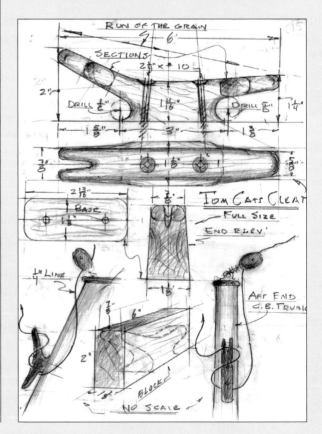

jambing. But a wooden cleat, as an alternative, in juniper or locust rather than bronze, would still outlast all of us.

Note on the cleat drawing, that the upper thumbs are angled outward to minimize the chance of a wrap, which could occur if simply slotting an existing conventional cleat. For the above work, a block of 1⅛" x 2" x 6", grain favoring as noted, is squared up. Holes are drilled, then the sides are beveled off. Next the profile is cut out, then the balance can be dressed off with a rasp and sanded into final finish. A couple of weeks in a pail of linseed oil, followed by drying and varnishing, will provide for long exposure.

For halyard cleats, simply omit the turned-up thumb. For deck cleats, up the size about 20%.

mast. An alternative, as on our Tom Cat, is to fit the mast with some sort of metal gooseneck. Ours was cobbled up from an old outhaul and some stuff from our hardware bins. A great variety of small-boat gear is available from the ship chandlers, but go with a fat wallet.

Sailcloth should be about 3.5-ounce Dacron which, when new, seems about as stiff as sheet metal compared to those lovely old cream-colored Egyptian cotton sails with their wonderful smell of tarred Italian hemp boltropes. Fit the sail with a single reef and three reef-points plus a clew and a tack cringle, and have a hook at the gooseneck to take the reefing tack cringle. To reef, all you have to do is to slacken the halyards, hook the tack, then secure the outhaul, tie off the three reefpoints to gather the bunt of the sail, then reset the halyards, and we're off with a rap-full.

"Lacing is so much simpler [than mast hoops] and can be gathered up as the sail is lowered by a thumb cleat…"

Have the sailmaker use good-sized grommets. You'll notice that Tom's sail is laced to the boom and gaff—and to the mast as well—with a simple lacing of 1/8" synthetic braid similar to seine twine. The outhaul is three parts of the same stuff. Be sure to leave enough slack in the foot lacing to let the roached foot flop over to leeward in light going. The Beetles' mast hoops have clever brass hanks that attach them to the luff of the sail, but hoops are an abomination on a small boat. Lacing is so much simpler and can be gathered up as the sail is lowered by a thumb cleat screwed to the forward side of the mast. Lacing is easy to adjust when underway as well. But for a sail that is to be

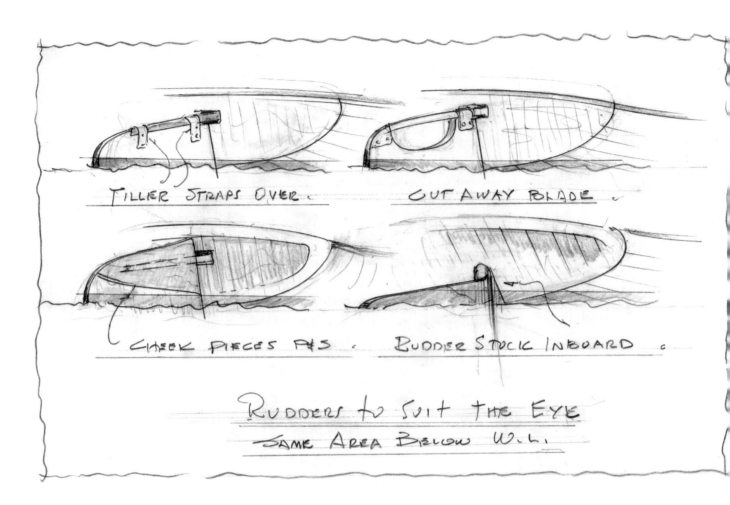

TILLER STRAPS OVER.   CUTAWAY BLADE.

CHEEK PIECES P&S .   RUDDER STOCK INBOARD .

RUDDERS TO SUIT THE EYE

SAME AREA BELOW W.L.

taken off and put in the bag after each use, the Beetle-type hoops plus sail track on the boom and gaff are mandatory.

> *"Often these little*
>
> *mouse-sized boats end up with*
>
> *sails requiring a strong hand…"*

You will get the best results from a sailmaker who is familiar with small gaff sails. Ask for the absolute minimum number of layers in the tabling buildup as well as the lightest acceptable sailcloth. Often these little mouse-sized boats end up with sails requiring a strong hand or a Billy-club to beat down the clew when furling, along with an outhaul doubling that's strong enough to handle the load of a 50-footer. And be sure and fit Tom with a sensitive masthead fly.

This, plus attention to the peak halyard and sail shape, will keep the boat in racing trim.

Both halyards are led aft to cleats or snubbing winches, with peak to port and throat to starboard in the time-honored way. The halyards are led aft over the cabin trunk, given a turn around the small snubbing winches, then over brass half-oval chafing pieces, and down to bulkhead-mounted cam cleats. The coiled halyards are stowed on bulkhead button cleats. Snubbing winches may seem unnecessary, but my friend Bill Page happened to have a pair of these of perfect size. For the peak halyard in particular, which needs frequent tweaking to keep the sail wrinkle-free, a snubbing winch is worthwhile.

You will probably think that this description is getting overdone by now. But I hope to be paid by the word, so bear with me.

continued on page 22 ➤

BOOM TENT

I've found that most boom tents and cockpit covers are so difficult to put on that often the job is postponed as not being worth the bother. Tom Cat's boom tent is simple to make and to install. It's formed along each side by a dowel, a length of bamboo, or an old whip antenna inserted into each fore-and-aft hem. To set the tent up, you unroll it and put the tip of one dowel into the transom block, bend it around the curved coaming (and under the coaming's finger rail), and fit the dowel's forward end under the clip on the inboard face of the forward toerail, then flop the tent and its opposite dowel over the boom and hook it as above and as per the sketch. When not in use, the tent is rolled up on the dowels like a window shade, then stowed forward in the cuddy or slung under the boom.

With the sail given a tight furl to hold it in place, it and the boom become the ridge-pole for the tent; the peak halyard and lazy-jacks are slacked off and the peak block slid forward on its bridle to clear the tent's forward edge. The tent's length allows it to overlap the cuddy enough to repel normal rain. Note that the aft end of the tent has a sock built into it to fit over the boom, while forward on the centerline is a grommet with a short pendant to tie to the gaff bridle's forward eye for stretching the tent's peak. Port and starboard amidships a short tab snaps over a dot fastener on the deck to provide security in a strong breeze.

Before the idea of a boom tent and the sleeping onboard sketch lead you off into dreams of cruising, it will be well to mock up the actual space available with the realization that while this might be sumptuous for a couple of kids overnight or somewhat acceptable for a pair of friendly sailors, it's a minimal cruiser's cocoon at best. As kids, my long-ago chum John Adams and I, at about age 12, made our first overnight cruise out of Port Madison, sleeping on the floorboards of a leaky, open jib-and-mainsail boat. The foray is remembered as a night of rolling at anchor and cold bilgewater, but mainly for a big rib-poking U-bolt coming up right in the middle of the floorboards. Kathy Bray, as a young Green's Island girl, is reported to have lived one summer onboard her moored Beetle Cat *Princess*. Tom Cat's accommodations, compared to this, would be approaching pure luxury.

To show the magnitude of calculations involved in our catboat project, we've even

BOOM TENT continued...

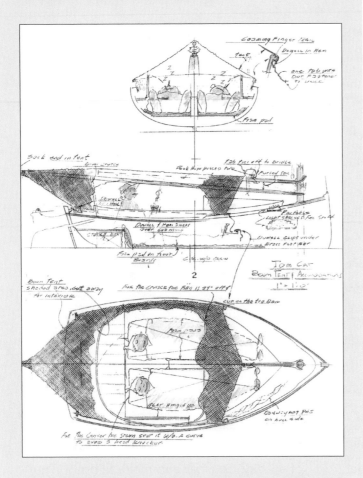

found the longitudinal center of gravity (LCG) of a sleeping crew and have assured ourselves that she won't trim by the stern with their heads downhill, the blood all staying aft and cold feet up forward. But take along a good pillow anyway.

The following sailing description may be a long time in the future for those considering becoming new Tom Catters, but will eventually be of some value.

In getting underway, hoist the sail with halyards gathered together as a single line, the gaff going aloft about horizontally. Then, when the throat is two-blocked, belay it and peak up the gaff as needed for good sail shape. In lowering the sail, some gaff angle will help, with the thrust of the gaff pushing down the sail's luff as the lacing is gathered by the thumb cleat mentioned earlier. The sail plan on page 12 shows line sizes and blocks to match.

> *"Like all small boats of rotund form, Tom Cat does best at a minimum angle of heel…"*

Like all small boats of rotund form, Tom Cat does best at a minimum angle of heel, so that the waterline remains more nearly symmetrical side-to-side. In light airs and flat sea, Tom will go to windward quite well with the centerboard raised, the lateral plane being provided by the 2"-deep keel, the sharp forefoot, and the big slab of a rudder. Helm then is about neutral, and having the centerboard up is handy for sliding across the kelp beds or skinning up along a beach. The center of effort then is about 12% forward of the center of lateral resistance if the rudder length is included, or 14% based on the waterline length of just the hull. With the board down, the CLR has an "on the wind" lead of about 10.6%, with the rudder lightly loaded and the tiller perhaps 1" off centerline in a nice sailing breeze. The board can be raised by a line that passes through a hole in the centerboard's tongue, then led forward to a lizard tied to the mast, then aft to a jamb cleat on the centerboard trunk. To hold the board down, a length of shock cord goes through the hole in the tongue with an eye on the other end that hooks over a thumb cleat aft on the trunk, providing just enough pull to hold the board down but allowing it to swing up in case it hits bottom. When sailing through kelp or heavy weed, the shock cord can be released so the board floats in a halfway-down position; that way it will more readily shed kelp. The sketches on page 17 and 18 will clarify the above.

Broad-reaching, in all the wind she can stand up to short of reefing, Tom's fat little hull can require some real helm. For our cat, I've used carbon fiber to stiffen up the narrow tiller where it slips between the rudder's cheek pieces. The usual catboat rudder, with strap yokes similar to those of a Beetle Cat, would accept a wider and stiffer tiller section without the complication of carbon fiber.

You will note that the side decks shown on the drawings are narrower than those in the photos of our own boat *Catspaw*. Tom Cat's decks have been narrowed to the minimum that's required to accommodate the planking, frames, and carlins. This results in an 8" wider cockpit for increased leg and knee room in way of the centerboard trunk, as well as a slightly greater righting moment due to the crew sitting farther outboard. Coamings on Tom have also been given increased rake for a more comfortable back

TRAVELER SKETCH TOM CAT

TRIED TWO MAIN SHEET HORSE LENGTHS
22" FIRST THEN THE 46" ONE WITH
A TRIMMING LINE TO ADJUST THE RUN OF
THE TRAVELER BLOCK IS BEST CHOICE

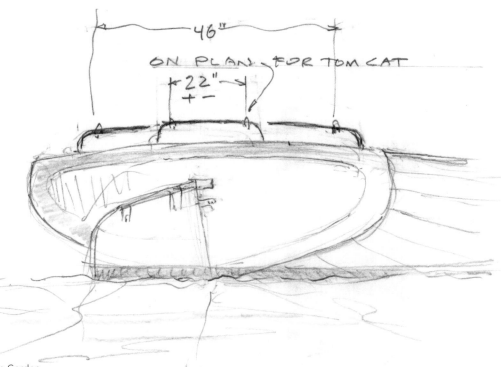

46"

ON PLAN FOR TOM CAT

22"
+ —

Curved Transom Option

If you wish to avoid going through the tedious graphical expansion of a curved and raked transom, a strongback can be fitted at the angle of the transom rake between the apron and the shop floor. A concave template of the transverse curve can then be made of, say, 3/8" plywood as shown on sheet 8, and laid across the ribbands with the template's centerline touching the strongback and its curve marked on each ribband to indicate the position of small blocks that will be screwed to the ribbands as guides or shoulder stops when bending and edge-setting the transom frame. After the frame has been bent and temporarily screwed to the ribbands, the frame and the ribband ends are beveled off to match the concave template of the curved transom. If a double layer of 1/4" plywood is used to form the transom, these pieces are bent over the centerline strongback and epoxied and screwed to the transom frame. Vertical stiffeners and a deckbeam will be fitted when she's turned right-side up and a centerline doubler added to take the rudder gudgeon bolts.

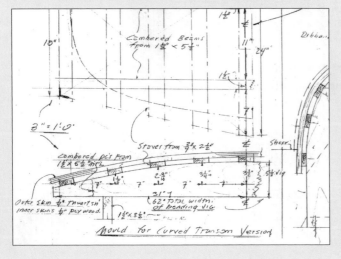

angle, and the seats are an inch higher with a slight tilt-up at their inboard edges. For overnighting, the seats can be built to hinge up out of the way so two could turn in on foam mattresses rolled out on each side of the centerboard trunk, their feet forward in the cuddy. With a tight boom tent, things couldn't be much better. Sternsheets are fixed, with space under them to take the ship's stores box.

BACK TO THE RIG

Always do a shipshape job of furling. So often a nice little boat has a furling job that looks as if its sail had been pushed into a wad by a ragman. It's a simple matter to let the sail, as it is lowered, fall on your side of the boom; then, with the gaff about parallel to the boom and held there by the peak halyard, pull the sail aft to straighten it along the boom. Then work from the peak down the leech, shaking and tucking the bunt into the hammock formed between the foot of the sail and the boom. Then secure it with a couple of sail-stops so it looks even and nicely tapered.

LAUNCHING CATSPAW

Our cat was ready to launch on August 4th, a little while after the Beetles arrived and after the usual boatbuilder delay. In defense, I offer a claim of the builder's having seen 84 summers at the time, plus having decided to make the boat more fancy than initially envisioned. In all, *Catspaw* eventually consumed about 700 man-hours. So it's a lot of labor despite its small size.

Catspaw was launched by swinging the hull out of the building shed and lowering away. Then she was paddled around to the float to step the mast, bend the sail, and generally put things in order ready for a proper flag-flying christening—an important sendoff for a small ship to instill in her the confidence to face the rolling deep. For the formal ceremony, scheduled next day, we fitted the building cradle with four 6" mine-car flanged wheels and, on the gravel beach, laid down a 25' track of 2x4s ballasted down with flat stones. A long plank temporarily placed across the head of our cove formed a seat for folks to sit and view the launching.

At high tide, we cradled the boat at the top of the ways so she'd be ready to launch at midday half tide and would have a good run

*"A rocket went up,
then Teri—our Beetle-owning
neighbor from Kolb Island
to the west of
us—broke the bottle
and christened her
Catspaw…"*

down the rails after the dog shore was knocked out. (Actually we cut a light line, but "dog shore" always sounds good.) When the time came for launching, four or five hundred folks had gathered (actually, it's more accurate to shed a zero off that estimate) to watch. A rocket went up, then Teri—our Beetle-owning neighbor from Kolb Island to the west of us—broke the bottle and christened her *Catspaw*, while Heather, our other Beetle neighbor from the island to the southwest, cut the line and let her go trundling down the ways. All went well that day, with Janie—my stalwart companion—onboard *Catspaw* to take over when afloat. Like clockwork, the wee boat and Janie rolled happily down to meet the tide. All this amid

thunderous cheers from those watching, and with the Beetles *Top Cat* and *Overture*, the old *Merlin* and miscellaneous other launches in attendance. "Offcut" Johnson's sloop (page 24 of *Yacht Designs*—incidentally, a book everyone should have and whose royalties help pay for my high living style) was there as well. Soon afterwards, we were off to the picnic spot… but first, let me tell you the saga of the christening bottle, one of this launching's many highlights.

This bottle of Atlantic seawater from Maine was flown out on Bill Page's lap after it had been ceremoniously blessed by "King Neptune" Bray on the beach in Brooklin, Maine, dressed his full regalia and aided by Page (backed up by Anne Bray and Paula Page to ensure protocol), checked for small lobsters and halibut fry, then formally surveyed and certified by Giffy Full. That ceremony was professionally filmed for posterity by the crack Australian camera crew of Ruth and Matthew Holliday. (The scene startled some folks retreating up the beach, and mutterings about "another cult" were overheard.) So much for the bottle; now back to the celebratory feast.

Louie Howland's grandfather wrote of some great clambakes in his book *Sou'west and by West of Cape Cod,* but his recipes seemed to take about a week to put together, so the christening ladies put on their own sumptuous spread with the centerpiece a 3'-long loaf of Italian grain bread rigged with a small cat mainsail at its forward end and surrounded by plates of chicken wings, crab legs, salads, things with little umbrellas over them, and a huge cake six stories (actually six layers) high with catboat-shaped icing, along with a couple of dozen dessert choices.

BUILDING HINTS

SOME HELPFUL THOUGHTS

START WITH SHARP TOOLS

SHARPENING TOOLS is a good way to return to the building of Tom Cat, with plane blades being first and foremost in importance. Next to not burning the temper out of the cutting edge by holding the blade too long against the grinder, is grinding the blade to an even angle. Having a good steady-rest on the grinder comes first, then a reference mark on the blade to ensure a constant angle at each sharpening. This is best accomplished by scratching a line across the back of the blade to indicate the position of the chip breaker which is turned over and clamped on the back of the blade and used as a grinding guide as shown in the sketch on page 28. For block planes, or blades without a chip breaker, the reference scratch-line can be matched up to a tool guide made from a 1½"-wide piece of 1/8" metal or plastic—length to suit blade width—that is clamped to the blade. For wooden backing-out planes with convex blades, or the blade of a concave spar plane, the tool rest can be ground to match the desired curve of the blade, secured to the back of the blade at the reference line (which, incidentally, must be reestablished over time as grinding obliterates it).

Keep your oilstone clean by wiping off the residue after each sharpening. WD-40 seems to be a worthwhile sharpening lubricant.

continued on page 28 ➤

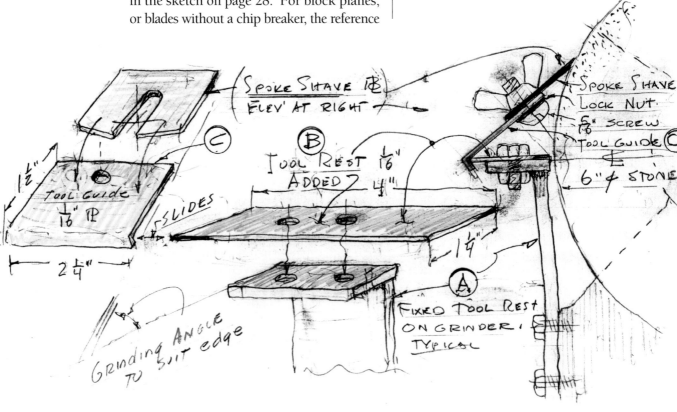

ON SPARS

A bit of Roy Campbell's poem "Choosing a Mast" will lead us into some helpful numbers relating to the sizing of Tom's mast and spars:

> New shaved, through whom I rive the ropes,
> says she was once an oread* of the slopes,
> graceful and tall upon the rocky highlands,
> a slender tree, as vertical as noon.

A tree and a mast standing without shrouds are both cantilevers that depend on their stiffness to resist breaking. With a catboat's narrow breadth at the mast partners, shrouds lack the needed spread at their base for effectiveness, so the time-honored pole mast, cantilevered from the bow, must have sufficient stiffness to carry the load of the sail. For a preliminary estimate of the mast diameter, the rule-of-thumb sizes of what has proven to work in the past are noted in the sketch bottom left.

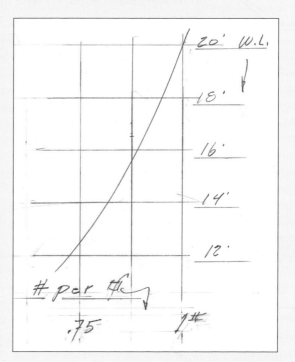

The above accompanying graph indicates the pounds per square foot of wind pressure for various waterline lengths (LWL).

For Tom Cat, the mast diameter at the deck is noted as .019 to .02 times its length from deck to the topmost band. Using .019, the diameter works out to be (.019)(171") = 3.249".

*Greek mountain nymph

Typ – Rule of Thumb – Cat Spars

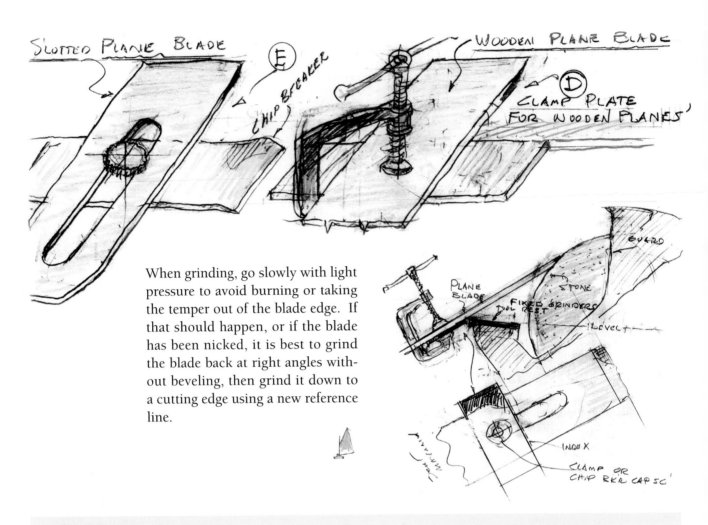

When grinding, go slowly with light pressure to avoid burning or taking the temper out of the blade edge. If that should happen, or if the blade has been nicked, it is best to grind the blade back at right angles without beveling, then grind it down to a cutting edge using a new reference line.

ON SPARS continued...

To check this, the diameter if Tom's mast be solid and calculated as a cantilever results in:

$$D = \sqrt[3]{16 \times .75 \times 120 \times 171 \times 3 \,/\, (3.14 \times 6700)} = 3.27''\text{ diameter}$$

Where 16	=	constant
.75	=	lb. per sq. ft. load for a boat of this size
120	=	sail area in sq. ft.
171	=	deck to peak halyard band (14.25 x 12)
3	=	safety factor
6700	=	allowable fiber stress for spruce (7800 lbs./sq.in. if Douglas-fir)

In the above calculation, the load and the safety factor are both at the minimum for a boat of this size to achieve the benefits of lightweight spars. Tom's *hollow* 3½" mast has stood well for the use we give her, but for stronger winds with a chance of dismasting and being blown offshore, it would be well to step a *solid* mast of 3½" diameter.

For those who wish to make a lighter, hollow mast of equivalent strength, its moment of inertia (M.I.) should be equal to or greater than that of the solid mast, that being:
M.I. = π (3.25)^4 /64 = 5.47 in^4. To develop the hollow mast, a couple of sections were sketched out and finalized at 3.5" O.D. with a core of 2.125". The resulting:
M.I. = π (3.5)^4 − (2.125)^4 /64 = 6.35 in^4.
The hollow mast's M.I. has been some-what larger than that of the solid mast to allow some variation in the wall thickness. Despite this stiffer section, the hollow mast is considerably lighter, weighing in at 1.12 pounds per foot against the solid mast's 1.67.

Note that halyard turning blocks or other fittings screwed to the mast contribute to stress concentration that can lead to a break, so it's best to only epoxy the boom jaw bolster and thumb cleat. Halyard turning blocks are fastened to the deck and kept 5" to 6" away, port and starboard, of the mast to avoid the halyards ending up fouled up in the gaff jaws and parrel trucks.

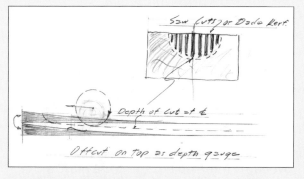

In shaping the hollow mast, the two halves are sawn to the correct taper; then, per the sketch above, the offcut shim from the

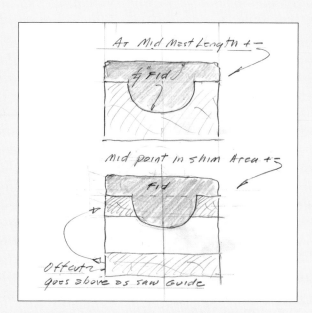

tapered side is tacked onto the opposite side as a depth guide for the handheld circular saw cuts in troughing out the core. Set the saw depth to allow about a 3/4" wall thickness, to be finalized at 11/16". A cardboard fid or template can be made as shown to establish the cuts. Think at least three times before you make each cut. If available, a convex spar plane will make quick work of the final hollowing. Once the core of both halves is sealed, the pieces can be epoxied and clamped together on a flat bench. After the glue dries, the mast is tapered, eight-sided, then sixteen-sided, and, finally, rounded off as shown on page 30.

For a solid mast, it's a good idea to cut and season a couple of trees for later choice. If a young tree is used, the diameter is net after allowing for dressing off the sapwood. First the tree is skinned of bark and sapwood with a slick or a spar knife, then a cut (with a handheld circular saw) is run

ON SPARS continued...

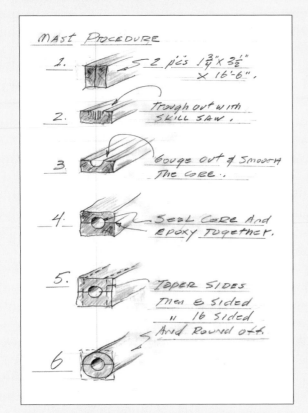

MAST PROCEDURE

1. = 2 pc's $1\frac{3}{4}$" x $3\frac{1}{2}$" x 16'-6".

2. Trough out with SKILL SAW.

3. Gouge out & smooth The core.

4. Seal core and epoxy together.

5. Taper sides Then 8 sided " 16 sided And Round off.

6.

lengthwise along one side into the center of the tree to allow it to dry with a minimum of checking. Give it a year or two to open up and season while the boat is being built, then epoxy a tapered wood wedge within the opened saw cut prior to dressing the mast down to its finished dimensions. A clear fir 4"x 4" (3½" x 3½" net) will be equally good, in which case the squared timber is planed to 3¼" x 3¼", then tapered per sheet 9, eight-sided, sixteen-sided, and rounded off with a hollow spar plane or with a jack plane, followed up with a block plane and a hollow sanding block to finish. Eight-siding the parallel section can be done on a planer by making a simple angle jig. The taper can then be worked down on the

bench. If the mast is to be finished bright, rough-round it, then finish with 80-grit paper on a hollow-faced block—sanding diagonally to fair up the round, then fore-and-aft with finer paper to suit. Hop to it, and the mast will be finished while the labor savers are figuring out some complicated way to do this simple job.

The boom and gaff can be tapered to the rectangular sections, then rounded off as shown (if round spars are preferred, proportional diameters are note on the Tom Thumb sketch, page 27) The gaff, you will note, has a peak halyard bridle to distribute the bending load on this spar. Simple stops for the bridle are epoxied on to fix its position. Gaff jaws are shown on sheet 9 and can be made from natural crooks or from laminated oak bent to the curve shown. The gaff parrel is of wire with the parrel trucks or wooden beads from a bead store, or simply sawn-off broomstick sections, drilled out, rounded off, and soaked in sealer, then varnished.

For a mast skirt, the little Beetles simply pop the mast into a fairly loose partner hole in the deck, the turned-in deck canvas forming somewhat of a cushion for the mast. The hole in Tom's partner is 1/4" larger in diameter than the mast, the fiberglass deck overlay is trimmed neat, and the mast is secured by a small wedge to rake it, then a fitted skirt of 3/8" plywood is screwed to the deck and painted the deck color.

THE SHOP

MOST ANY SPACE WILL DO for a shop if it can accommodate a 12' x 6' boat with 6' extra length at the ends and space along the sides for a 2'-wide workbench plus 4' clear working space on the bench side and another 4' from the boat to the wall opposite. The shed as sketched—about 20' long and 23' wide with 7'6" of headroom—would be pure luxury, but boats have been built in far smaller spaces. Living rooms, upstairs bedrooms, and endless varieties of garages and basements have all produced good boats; however, there is something about an unused barn that always gives me the urge to step it off to see what keel length would fit. And what a great place to build a boat—with gables of quiet, interested spiders looking on, swallow nests up in the rafters, and rough walls to nail up old molds plus racks for spars

continued on page 33 ➤

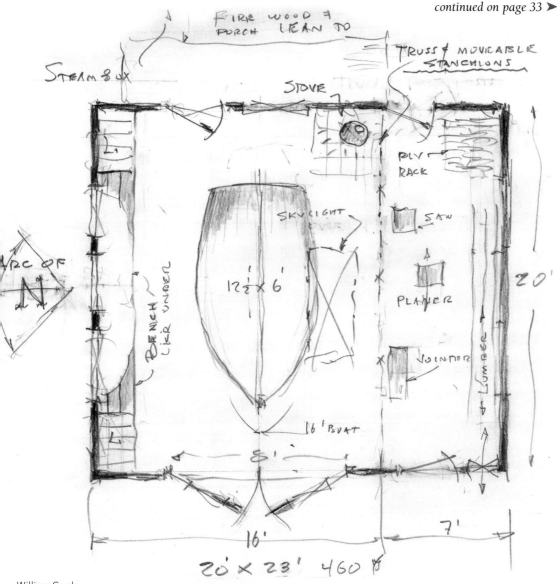

CATSPAW'S BUILDING SHED

Our own boat would be considered a silver-spooner, having been "bornded," as the Beetles have enviously said, in pure luxury having a choice of several berths in either of our two shops with old "Doc" Bill in full-time attendance.

The Toad's Landing shop has grown over 35 years from an open fisherman's net shed of 22' x 39' (the present lower shop) to a 79' x 28' upper shop with a machine room between the two. Lots of roofs to keep up, but wonderful space for small boats. The lower shop was chosen for building our Catspaw since it had a southern window wall for some winter sun. A furnace or heating stove is of questionable worth in an old building full of knotholes and cracks, but is enough to break a winter chill. The original 3" x 12" deck in this shop has been floored over with plywood to form a good lofting base. A bench runs along under the windows, producing a glare when working there on sunny days, but it's a cheery place to work withal.

Our 9" bandsaw is a portable and neat little tool. For some reason the 59½" blades on these saws seem to be of better metal than those on our 14" saw in the upper shop. As with all of these portable woodworking tools, the initial cost for a one-boat job can be somewhat reimbursed by eventual resale. An advertisement selling a used planer, saw, drills, or whatever always seems to attract a quick buyer— a point worth bringing up when faced by the wrath of Momma.

Over in our shop's northeast corner is a good drill press and metalworking equipment, then along the north wall is an array of (high-class) marine stuff—referred to as junk by the unknowing. The southeast corner is devoted to painting and paint storage shelves, while in the southwest corner hang the tools for the marine ways, clamps, jacks, bars, etc. At the moment, on a shelf just inside the door, is an Oregon junco's annual nest, with Mrs. Snowbird busy dashing in and out and giving us lip while getting bug snacks for her chicks.

Alongside and to the south of this lower shop is a 20-ton marine railway powered by a 3-h.p. electric motor driving, via a belt, an old truck rear end's gearbox attached to the winch drum. Forty-pound rails and 6"-diameter double-flanged turntable wheels from a purse seiner carry the cradle's load.

Up some steps from the lower shop is an open-sided area with racks for lumber and for small boats on one side, a tablesaw in the middle, plus the third bandsaw which is belt-driven off the line shaft. Off in the back and lumber, all coupled with the fragrance of new-cut wood and great big sliding doors to open on the sunny days. A barn like this would be great, but a double garage would also have room for one of today's neat little thickness planers, a jointer, a 14" bandsaw, and the usual shop accumulation of good things. On the smaller shop side, *WoodenBoat* has run articles on simple boat sheds of bent plastic pipe and plastic tarps. A rough-

> *"For a small-sized shop a portable car shelter could also do, with your building jig on casters…"*

framed shed with a plastic tarp cover [the gothic arch sheds devised by David Stimson that are covered with greenhouse plastic are one good example—Eds.] and an adjacent basement set up for bad weather days would also do the job, but to put the family car out in the wet for two or three years is reasonably sure to put a dent in family harmony. A neat reminder sign in the shop to the effect that working on a boat is better than sitting on a bar stool also might help. For a small-size shop a portable car shelter could also do, with your building jig on casters so the boat can be rolled out for real elbow room or for turning over after planking—but best of all would be to put up a proper shed that can later be used for garden tools or storage.

HANDLING AND LAUNCHING

For handling a Tom Cat in and out of the water, the most practical method is by a boat ramp with a galvanized boat trailer. Then off home for the winter. For hoisting, a loop sling can be made up with each end shackled into the eyebolts port and starboard of the mast. With the rudder off, the bight of the

BUILDING SHED continued...

end is the engineroom with a 1950s Vauxhall gas engine powering the overhead line shaft which drives, by belt, the heavier woodworking machines. The belt slap and line-shaft rumble form a pleasant recollection of boatshops of the 1930s. A belt-drive setup doesn't make sense today, considering the variety of electrically driven equipment available. When building this shop in the late 1960s, however, the island lacked shore power—so junkyard cruising unearthed lots of treasures to put back to work. A neat 40-ton steam shovel, I remember, was a hard bargain to resist.

But back to the shop. The line-shaft drive engine runs in second gear, turning a 12"-diameter pulley and a 24'-long, 6"-wide flat leather belt up to a 32" x 12" wooden bull-wheel mounted on the main 2" x 30' overhead line-shaft—its belts dropped down to drive the big bandsaw plus a 14" x 7'-long jointer, a 12" x 24" thickness planer, and a power hacksaw. All together, our shop holds about two tons of relics from small mills and woodworking shops of the past century—relics with countless busy turns already on their wheels, and pleased, I'm sure, with the smell of newly cut wood and the rhythmically musical slappety-slap of the traveling belts.

Nowadays, the alternative for this kind of stuff would be the cutting torch and reincarnation via the melting pot into something as dull, perhaps, as a roll of chicken-wire or a bundle of rebar.

continued on page 35 ➤

loop then goes out through the forward side of the rudderport, to be held by a piece of timber stuck through the loop and laid across the transom. Since our boat spends summers afloat, the dock boom provides a quick lift to scrub the bottom or to put her up for a mid-season bottom painting.

TOWING

Now something on towing. Prior to our immigrants' arrival, my examination of genus Beetle had been cursory and made during occasional visits to Beetle country in the East. Somewhere I had heard that Beetles don't like to be towed—which, in passing, seemed odd for such a hull form. Then the two Beetles arrived somewhat subdued from their long trip, one quite watertight while *Overture*, which had been neglected, was barely able to float. But overboard they went. *Ovie* had a barrel of water in her by the time we put the short towline through her mast partner to get her out to the island shop, and was moved out through the marina at a dead-slow bell. Then the poor little Beetle just plain rolled over—suicidal, it seemed—from the embarrassment of hearing the disparaging remarks of some dockside loafers. Anyway, she had no towing eye down low on the stem to bring

her head up, and this contributed to her temporary demise.

A good towing eye is a must for any small boat or dinghy—as low down as practicable, close to the water, to keep the bow up. A small cat, if towed with crew onboard, should have the tow line run through a proper towing eye, then on aft to belay near the hand of her crew. In case of trouble, such as a cowboy in command of the towboat, the line is quick to let go. For towing an empty boat, the tow line passes through the eye, then up through the chock, and belays to the mast.

"When towed faster than about six knots, Tom's centerboard trunk must be covered with a fitted cap..."

You'll locate the hole 2" to 4" up from the waterline, though the stem, for towing. It's a 7/8" hole lined with 7/8" O. D. copper tubing softened by annealing so that its end can be flared out. One end is flared, then the piece is inserted through the hole in epoxy and the other end peened into a flare with a grommet punch.

When towed faster than about six knots, Tom's centerboard trunk must be covered with a fitted cap on a soft gasket to keep the water from spurting through and gradually filling (and possibly capsizing) the boat. The trunk is already capped at its aft end, so, for towing, a simple removable snap-on cover can be fitted around the projecting vertical arm of the centerboard. If, for some reason, you do find her half full of water on the end of a towline, the towboat's speed should be reduced gradually to lessen the forward surge of the bilgewater, which could result in a broach or a capsize.

In open water when running off before the wind and sea with Tom Cat on the end of a tow line, and wanting to surf up on you on the back of a following sea, it's well to have a second line from the towboat, carried slightly slack, to the catboat's stern that can be thrown overboard to trail out behind as an efficient drogue.

MORE ON BOAT HANDLING

Because running Tom up the beach will prove to be a real load for four good men, it's best to moor the boat just offshore by dropping a light anchor, with buoy, on the way in, and rig an outhaul line running from the boat through a lizard or fairlead on the anchor buoy, and pay it out while coming on to the beach. After unloading, a retrieving line is rigged from the boat's stern to the shore, as shown on the sketch on pages 4 and 5.

WINDING UP

So that's about it, and off to the editors' unerring blue pencil and paste pot to put it all in shape. This morning the Beetles are busily getting their gear together over on Kolb Island under Peter's watchful eye. Our *Catspaw* is in equally good spirits out back in the slings, looking forward to a wet bottom again and heading off to windward with a nice ebb to boost her out the channel into a bright morning's sparking southeaster. But before you start building such a time-consuming little boat, think long and hard about the cuts and bruises ahead. *Despite such concerns, you'll find there isn't a megayacht in the world to equal the pleasure to be found in one small catboat!*

BUILDING SHED continued...

If you haven't already looked around enough at *Catspaw*'s birthplace, the big shop is yet to come, this one a shed on log framing of 28' x 36' with 18' of clear height, plus an extension on the east end of 20' x 40' with 14' overhead clearance. A set of launching ways extends 80' out of this east end. The cradle here is powered by a 5-h.p., three-phase electric motor located in a donkey-winch shed out back.

The belt-driven tools here consist of the big jointer, bandsaw, planer, and power hacksaw. There are also the usual electric tools—a small planer, jointer, sanders—and, as in the lower shop, lots of hand tools. Some racoons sleep up under the roof timbers but bail out if the line shaft starts to turn.

These shops might seem huge for a retirement operation, but they always seem full of boats and stuff, old engines, paint, lumber, and bins of nails, bolts, and screws. I count at the moment nine small boats, five new window boxes to go up on the house this week, and an endless "to do" list with three launches presently afloat and ready for their spring haulout and *Catspaw* ready to launch. It's a 3,000-sq.-ft. homemade heaven for a boat nut.

PERFORMANCE

COMPARING TOM CAT WITH A BEETLE

SOME DESIGN NUMBERS are needed and are of interest even in the development of such small boats. In this case, a simple comparison was made with the Beetles, since they would be the usual boats we would be sailing with. Variations of proportions in a 12' x 6' boat shape are limited, but our higher freeboard and added structure results in a L x B x depth—or volume—of hull increase of about 1.6 times that of Beetle, Tom being some 250 pounds more boat. The increase in size is readily apparent with the boats hauled out side by side. (the drawing from page 52)

Further comparison indicates the righting arms of the two designs close to equal; Tom's heavier displacement, however, results in a greater righting moment that more nearly matches Tom's 120 sq. ft. sail area to that of the Beetle's 112.

Tom's wetted surface is slightly higher due to the somewhat greater water plane area of the heavier boat, plus the area of Tom's exposed keel. However, the sail area–to–wetted surface ratio of the boats—the measure of a good drifter—is close.

To back up a bit, Tom's weight, in sail-away trim without crew, is 644 pounds. The Beetle's weight is about 400 pounds. Both are butterfly boats requiring a live crew to keep them upright in a breeze. When two 150-pound crew members are added to each boat for the under-sail study, the righting moment is about the same. Another comparison with the Beetles is the ratio of the square root of the sail area to the cube root of the displacement, which for the Beetle results in a ratio of:

$$\frac{\sqrt{112}}{\sqrt[3]{700}} = 1.19$$

From 1.10 to 1.25 seems a fair range for a good drifter, so the Beetle's 1.19 indicates a lively little boat. Checking Tom, we get

$$\frac{\sqrt{120}}{\sqrt[3]{944}} = 1.11$$

This is a lower number than the Beetle's 1.19, but close enough to be acceptable.

Further insight assumes that the sail area in square feet of similar boats varies as the 2/3 power of their displacement in cubic feet. Tom's sail area, then, to match that of the Beetle, is found by calculating:

$$112 \times \frac{(944/64)^{2/3}}{(700/64)^{2/3}} = 112 \times \frac{(6.02)}{(4.93)} = 112 \times 1.22 = 137 \text{ sq. ft.}$$

The sail area of 120 sq. ft. was chosen as a better visual match to the Beetle's sail plan. For our local voyaging it works out well, but one day I'll set a main of 137 sq. ft. to exactly match that of the Beetle's SA/Disp. ratio of 1.19 just to see how she goes.

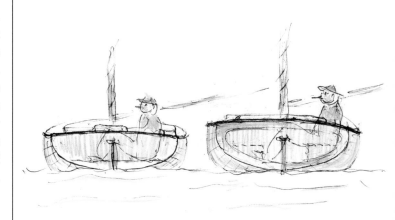

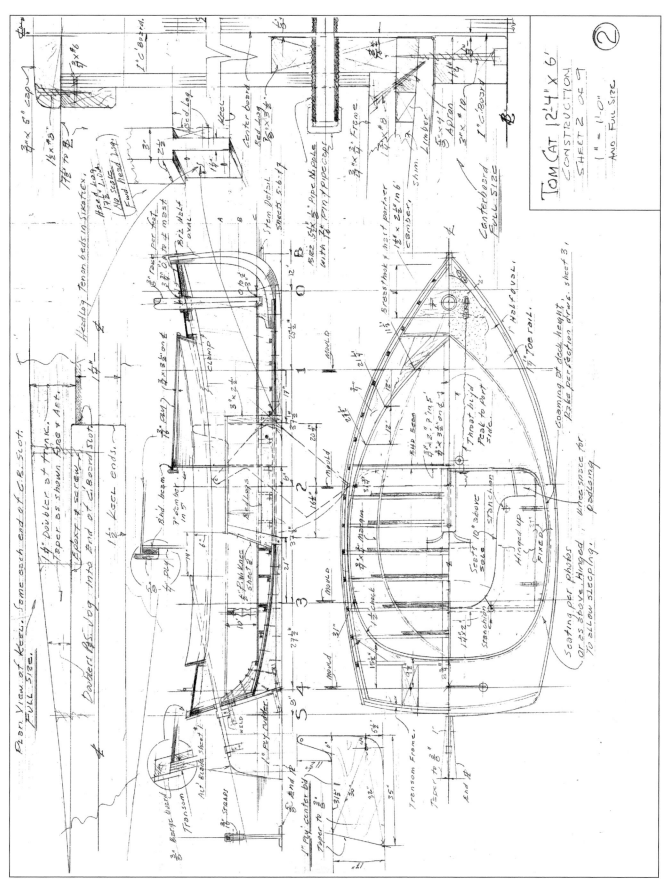

Sheet #1 is shown on page 12.

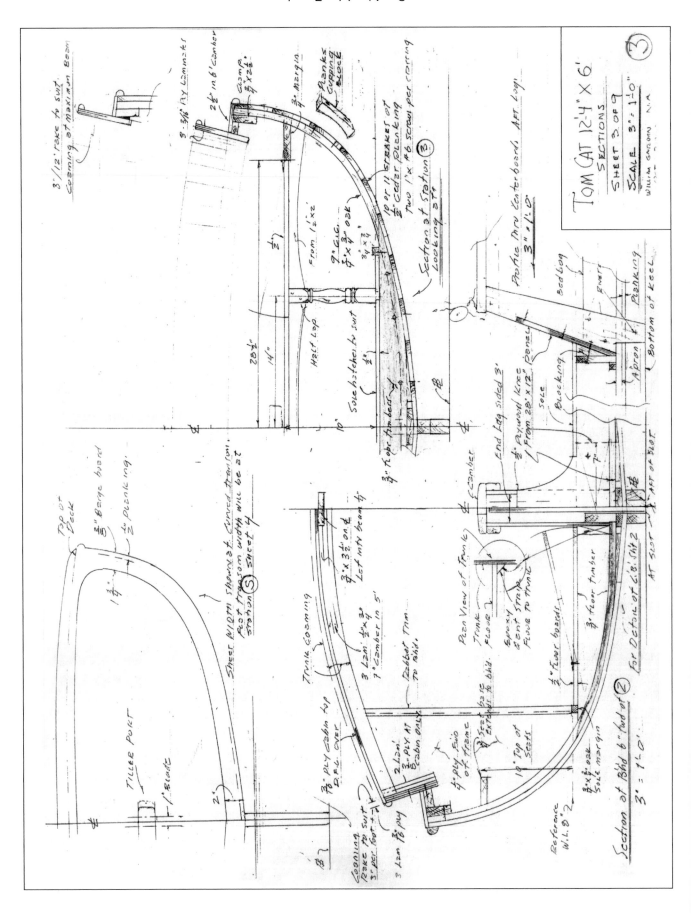

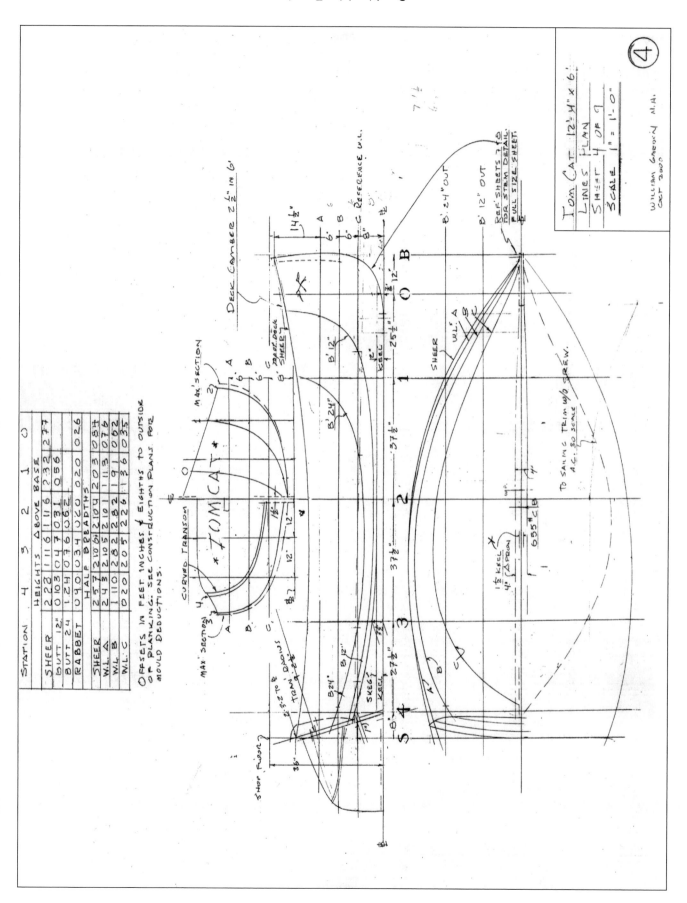

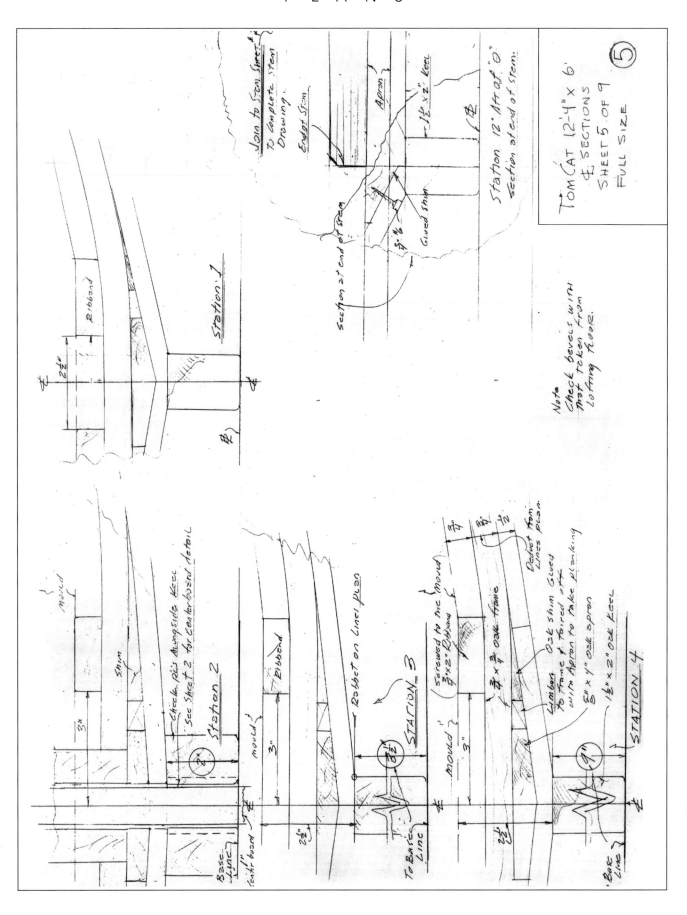

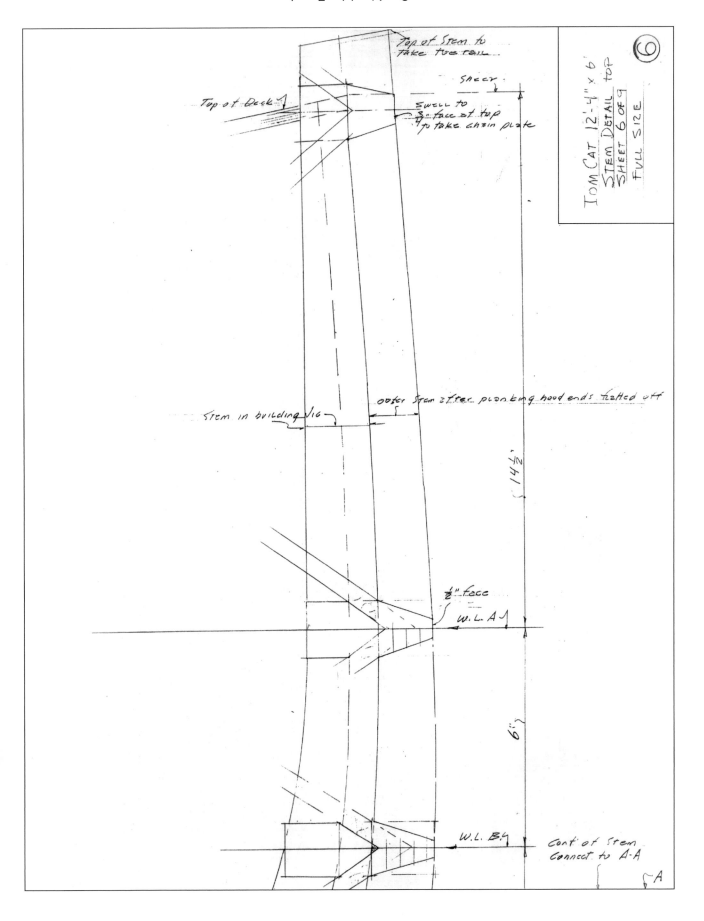

Top of Stem to
take toe rail

Sheer.

Top of Deck

Swell to
3" face at top
to take chain plate

Iom Cat 12'-4" x 6'
Stem Detail top
Sheet 6 of 9
Full Size

⑥

outer stem after planking hood ends fazed off

Stem in building ¹⁄₁₆

14½"

⅞" face
W. L. A

6"

W. L. B.

Cont. of Stem
Connect to A·A

A

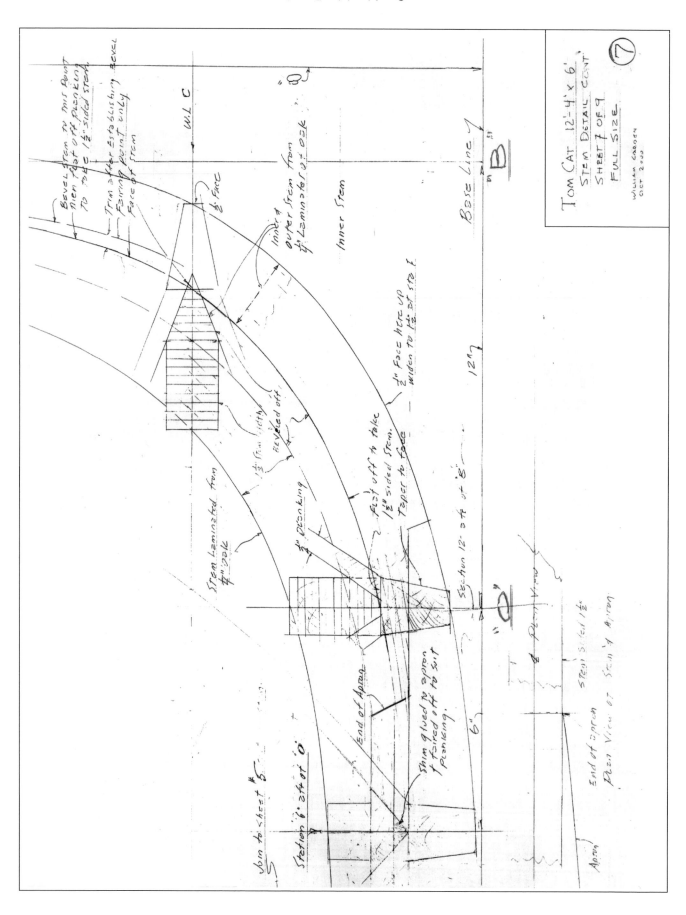

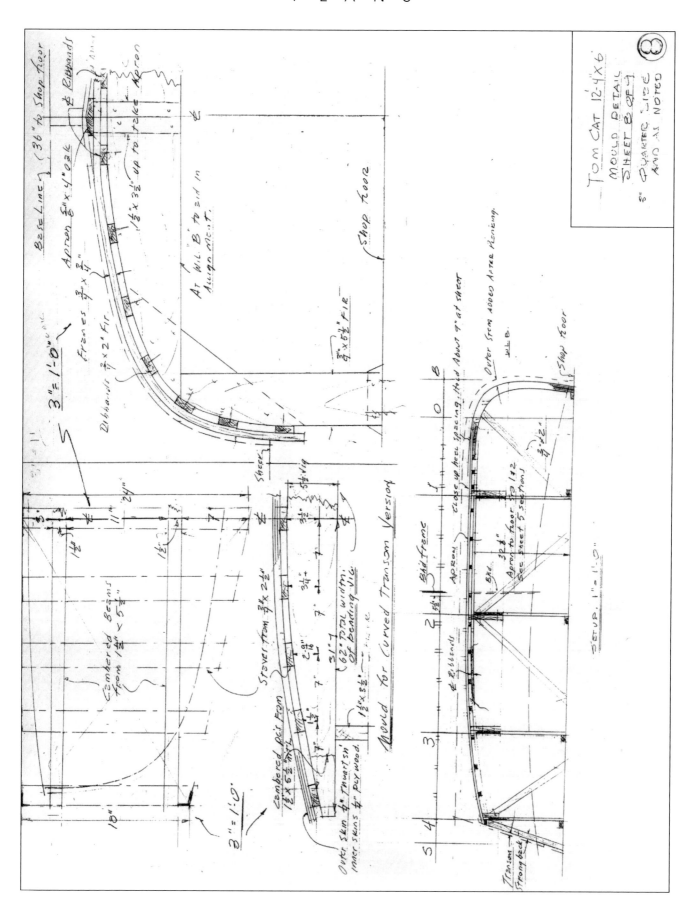

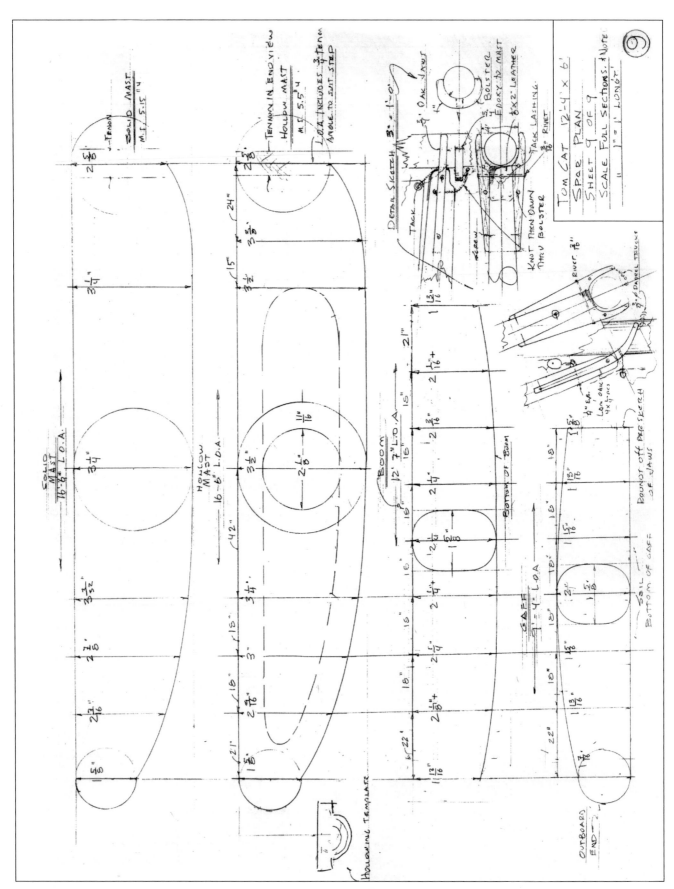

Please note, you may order the plan sets directly from The WoodenBoat Store, PO Box 78, Brooklin, Maine 04616.
800-273-SHIP (7447) www.woodenboatstore.com

The large and the small of it: examples of Bill Garden's vast scope. He designed the 164' motoryacht Evivva for his friend Orin Edson, and drew up and built Catspaw, the first Tom Cat, for himself.

A small cuddy was added for Catspaw's second season, giving her an even more distinctive look. It is depicted on the drawings for builders who wish to include this enhancement.

Good visibility comes from the high boom. The halyards lead to snubbing winches for fine-tuning underway. The peak halyard, especially, influences the set of the sail.

Tom Cat's hull is best built upside down, then turned over for completion. The frames near the bow, known as cant frames, fan out so they more or less equally fill the space as they run from stem to sheer.

Planking Tom Cat is made easier because of there being no stem rabbet. The planks can simply run out beyond the inner stem, then be trimmed off later to provide landing for the outer stem.

Bill's steam generator is a copper coil, fired by a propane flame, the nozzle for which is shown here alongside the furnace, rather than in it, for clarity.

The ribbands, over which the frames are bent, lay over the molds. Since the lines plan delineates the hull to the outside of the planking, deductions for plank, frame, and ribband thickness have to be made to establish the outline of the station molds. Except at the bow, the freshly steamed frames run from sheer to sheer.

A so-called Boston Scale helps establish the width of each new plank at each station by graphically dividing the remaining space into proportional parts.

Bill Garden planked this first Tom Cat carvel, after which he gave the entire hull a coat of clear, un-thinned epoxy. Then, instead of caulking with cotton and priming and puttying the seams, he filled the seams flush with thickened epoxy. The screw holes were given the same treatment.

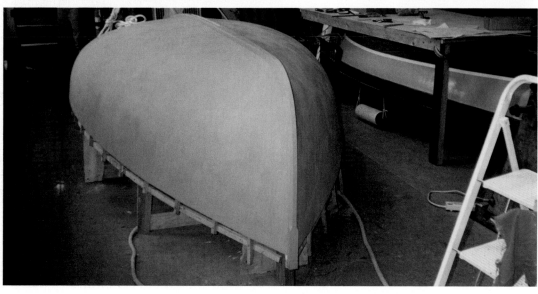

Biaxial cloth, laid in epoxy, covers the hull to protect the soft cedar planking against abrasion and keep it from soaking up water. This sheathing goes on after the keel and outer stem.

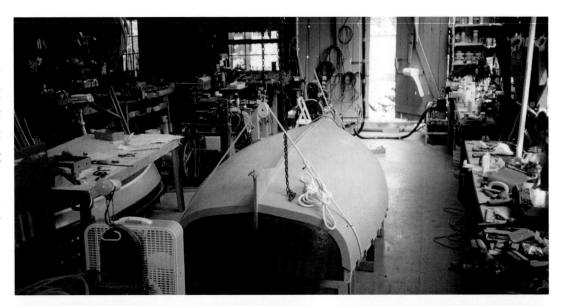

Here, the entire assembly, building jig and all, is about to be turned over. Slings at bow and stern hang from chainfalls, enabling their load, once lifted, to be easily rolled right-side up.

Once upright, the jig can be hoisted clear of the hull, as is being done here, so the interior can be completed. The centerboard slot is cut before the exterior is sheathed, enabling the sheathing to be turned down to cover the lower edges of the slot.

Tom Cat's interior work begins with the sheer clamps, quarter knees, deckbeams, and the floorboard margins and supports.

The floors, seats, centerboard trunk posts, and cockpit margin pieces go in next. For additional seating comfort, a wider cockpit is indicated on the drawings from what shows here.

Lots of C-clamps keep pressure on the curved, three-layer coaming lamination while the glue cures. In its first iteration, Bill's Catspaw was decked over all the way back to the cockpit. Later, the portion of deck inside the coaming was cut away for the cabin.

To keep the rudder shallow yet effective, an end plate was added to the bottom of it. In Catspaw, the tiller is inserted between cheeks that are glued along the upper part of the rudder and projects through an opening in the transom. But, as the sketch on page 20 shows, a number of other options are possible.

Catspaw's *curved transom rises above the deck, which enables a sculling notch to be cut into it. The transom is outlined by 2"-wide barge boards for a classier look as well as to cover the sheathing's ragged edge.*

She's a real little ship, Catspaw is, with all sorts of custom detailing.

You can see here how the mast-mounted thumb cleat gathers the luff lacing when the sail is lowered. The halyards lead aft along the cabintop to be within easy reach for underway adjustment.

As we sail along with the Beetlers sitting down there on the floorboards, we find that our Tom Cat, with its sheltering freeboard, old-money varnish, comfortable foam seat cushions, and padded backrests, has the pleasant aura of a golden age, lacking only the forbidden cigar of yesteryear. For the young and limber, however, the Beetle's simplicity and easy upkeep would tip the scales Beetle-wise.

William Garden